The Entrepreneur's Guide To Building <u>Real</u> Wealth

SALES VELOCITY

How To Sell More With Less Resistance

A <u>Proven</u> Three-Step Formula for Transforming
Your Business & Accelerating Your Profits

ANDREW J. CASS

Published by Best Seller Publishing®, Pasadena, CA
Best Seller Publishing® is a registered trademark
Printed in the United States of America.
ISBN-13: 978-1540587480
ISBN-10: 1540587487

This publication is designed to provide accurate and authoritative information with regard to the subject matter covered. It is sold with the understanding that the publisher is not engaged in rendering legal, accounting, or other professional advice. If legal advice or other expert assistance is required, the services of a competent professional should be sought. The opinions expressed by the authors in this book are not endorsed by Best Seller Publishing® and are the sole responsibility of the author rendering the opinion.

Most Best Seller Publishing® titles are available at special quantity discounts for bulk purchases for sales promotions, premiums, fundraising, and educational use. Special versions or book excerpts can also be created to fit specific needs.

For more information, please write:
Best Seller Publishing®
1346 Walnut Street, #205
Pasadena, CA 91106
or call 1(626) 765 9750
Toll Free: 1(844) 850-3500
Visit us online at: **www.BestSellerPublishing.org**

Praise For Sales Velocity...

"You will benefit greatly from Andrew Cass' book *Sales Velocity*, and will probably want to insist that employees and associates read it, especially if they came up in the Internet era. Andrew has been tremendously successful in the decade *Before The Internet* and in the decade *Of The Internet*. He knows the fallacies of abandoning pre-Internet media for online-only media, understands the integrated approach I champion, and is well qualified to lead you to *selling more.*"

- **Dan Kennedy:** Multi-millionaire serial Entrepreneur, direct marketing strategy consultant, and author of the popular No B.S. book series including the *No B.S Guide To Sales Success In The New Economy*

"Andrew Cass was part of my Inner Circle years back. He definitely knows what he's doing and he understands the importance of sales funnels at a very high level. His book Sales Velocity is a road map anyone can follow to better organize and streamline their sales process from front to back. This is one of the must-read sales books out there today and it will definitely give your sales a big boost which, of course, will make you more money."

- **Russel Brunson:** Author of the USA Today and Amazon Best Selling book, *DotCom Secrets: The Underground Playbook For Growing Your Business Online, and Founder of ClickFunnels*

"I just added an extra $250,000 in revenue to my bottom line from ONE webinar implementation idea Andrew Cass gave me. Thanks would be an understatement. Our company has doubled in revenue EVERY year since being a part of his Inner Circle. In 2015 and 2016 we landed on the **Inc. 5000 List** of fastest growing privately held companies in the US, and these trainings, these philosophies Andrew teaches and writes about have been a big part of our success."

- **RJon Robins:** Founder of *How To Manage A Small Law Firm*, an Inc. 5000 company - the leading, largest, biggest and best provider of outside Managing Partner, Chief Operating Officer (COO) and Chief Financial Officer (CFO) services exclusively for the solo and small law firm (single-shareholder) market

"Andrew and I go back a long way. We worked closely together in a Direct Sales company years back where we became top producers and friends. He is the real deal and his book Sales Velocity comes at the perfect time. It's one of few sales books I know of that stresses the importance of using BOTH pre-Internet and post-Internet tools. Very few grasp the importance of being this well rounded today. Read this book."

- **Mike Dillard:** Author, Entrepreneur, Founder of the #1 self-help podcast on iTunes, *Self Made Man*

"I implemented ONE idea Andrew spoke about at one of his sales training seminars in Miami and I booked three new resume clients in one day! It wound up giving me the extra revenue to put me over $11k in sales this month, making it my best month yet since leaving the legal world. Thanks!"

- **Wendi Weiner:** The Writing Guru, Forbes Career Coach, Huffington Post Contributing Writer

"Our company grew from ZERO in 2011 to $1.1 Million in 2013, over $2 Million in 2014, and just about $3 Million in 2015. We were elected to the Inc. 5000 List of America's fastest growing companies in 2016 and Andrew's mentorship and being part of his 7-Figure Mastermind group had a big impact on our growth. If you have the opportunity to join his Inner Circle, read his book, or get access to this type of high-level training, you really should. Andrew is brilliant and will help you see your business in a completely different light."

- **Josh Nelson:** Co-Founder of Plumbing & HVAC SEO - the leading Internet marketing agency in the United Sates for plumbing and HVAC companies.

"Someone once said, nothing happens until you sell something. These words are more relevant today than ever. Selling is an essential skill, and inside the pages of this book you will learn the art of selling from a seasoned pro. Andrew knows how to sell; face-to-face, to groups, on the phone, and on webinars. He sells products, services, himself, his clients… he knows how to sell. Inside this book he gives you a formula that works for him and his clients. Study this book, it will help you close more sales and make more money."

- **Brian Kaskavalciyan:** Serial entrepreneur, co-founder of The Wealthy Contractor Program™ and author of *How to Double Your Profits in Six Months or Less.*

"Highest recommendation for Andrew Cass' book *Sales Velocity.* As an avid reader (I am a publisher after all) I am always intrigued by the latest idea or concept, often promoted by those doing 'research' or taking a deep dive into various aspects of the desired subject. This is NOT that kind of approach. The more my business grows the more I appreciate those with real world skills who are doing "IT" now. That is what this book brings to you. I've known Andrew for many years, having first met him as part of his mastermind group in Miami, FL. Andrew breaks down for the reader the exact steps that are working now in his business and have been proven over time to work in any business. As they say, *'nothing moves until something is sold',* so do yourself a favor and follow the strategies outlined is this excellent read."

- **Rob Kosberg:** #1 Best Selling author, Founder of Best Seller Publishing

Table of Contents

Acknowledgments & Dedication...

To my Dad, who supported me and encouraged me at all times, through every business endeavor since my teenage years, and who never missed one of my games growing up as a kid.

To my Mom, who always pushed me a little bit further than I thought I could go.

To my amazing children, my true gifts, Nicolas and Alessia, who are the driving force behind all I do.

To Dan Kennedy, who has been an instrumental sales and marketing advisor and mentor to me for the last decade.

Thank you.

My Mission

To show Entrepreneurs & Small Business Owners how to implement targeted lead generation campaigns and high-converting sales funnels for maximum profit.

- Andrew J. Cass

Introduction:

What If Everything You Have Ever Been Taught About *Selling* Is Wrong?

Hi, I'm Andrew Cass. Welcome inside Sales Velocity! We're in for quite a journey together…

Let me take the above question one step further…

What if everything you have ever been taught about selling is wrong <u>and</u> is costing you money?

Now do I have your attention?

It may be true. Keep reading, and you will learn the answer to that question. This book is based on my *two decades* of experience in the sales and marketing world, both before the rise of the Internet and during the Internet revolution. I call them the *old-school* days and the *new-school* days. In combining and refining the best practices from both eras, I've developed the *Sales Velocity* formula, a 3-part system that has <u>proven</u> successful time and again for selling in the New Economy <u>certain</u> to transform your business and accelerate your profits. I am not talking theory here. I'm sharing with you what actually works, today, inside some of the most profitable business models in the world…

The *Sales Velocity* formula may seem controversial to some and provocative to others, but the results are real. This book is based on my twenty hard-earned years of live, belly-to-belly sales experience, both offline and online, reaching 7-figures in production on three separate occasions before the age of forty two.

This book also calls out the *wanna-be* sales trainers and authors who write sales books with no real sales experience to back up their claims. Unfortunately, many sales books are not based on much real world experience today but rather, on studies. Shocking, I know.

You'll learn about the formulas and systems that work today, not what might have worked in a study group four years ago. You should ask yourself if you'd rather learn from a group of academics that have never sold much in their lives, or someone with experience-based selling results who can tell you what *really* works today...

This book is for small-business owners, entrepreneurs, and sales professionals. I lay out a proven three-step system on how to "sell more with less resistance." I call it *Sales Velocity* because it's more than just about the speed of the sale; it's about building sales systems with a clear and focused sense of direction. Before these 3-steps can produce results, however, a business must be clear about it's purpose and it's goals, and it must identify what makes it truly *unique* and *attractive*. We'll dive into that as a foundation in Part 1.

Each section of the book focuses on one of the three pieces of the *Sales Velocity* system. I actually view them as "laws" that must be *enforced* or selling is met with great *resistance*. They are laws for success, and as such, they must be enforced. I lay them out in exact order, the only order that truly brings results, and the order that is <u>critical</u> for attracting better customers, clients or members.

In the chapters to come, you will see examples of businesses or clients that I've worked with personally who have doubled or tripled their sales by integrating these concepts. You'll also enjoy a quote at the beginning of each chapter from the late, great Zig Ziglar, the person who rang in my ears on my very first sales training cassette tape back in 1995, when I began my sales career, at the age of twenty-one.

Finally, the *Sales Velocity* system isn't designed to just *make some money* for you. It's designed to create *leverage* "in your business" so that *real wealth* can be created "from your business." This will ultimately give you more freedom to lead the life you've always wanted.

As the saying goes: "systems will set you free." You become the *money person* when you have such systems for acquiring customers and dealing with them effectively. This book is designed to make <u>you</u> the money person in your business for years to come.

I've reserved a special invitation for you to register for my Sales Mastery Boot Camp on page 120. No need to wait until the end of the book to learn more about this powerful, advanced sales training, which is essentially Sales Velocity *on steroids*... ;)

First, a quick, yet important back story about how we got here and why I *may* be the most qualified to write about this topic and lead you to more sales...

The Author's Story:

Why I *May* Be The Most Qualified To Lead You To More Sales...

I guess you could say I've been selling *me* my whole life. I've always been persistent even back as early as elementary school...

I played sports my whole life – soccer, hockey, baseball, football, lacrosse – but it was football that I ultimately committed to. When I was fourteen years, I told my parents that I wanted to go to one of the top high schools in Boston, Massachusetts - Xaverian Brothers High School - and play on their top ranked Division 1 football team. They were shocked. I was small, somewhat fast, and not really that good. The local public school, a Division 5 football program, probably would have been just fine.

I went, but I got cut from the freshman football team, and had to play on a local Pop Warner football team with kids a year younger than me. I was crushed. It was embarrassing. I was down, but not out. I got to work, lifted the weights, got a bit better and faster, came back and played on the Junior Varsity team as a sophomore. I was a wide receiver.

I got a little bigger and faster and played again as a junior. This time, I got to travel with the Varsity team. By my senior year in high school, I was bigger, faster, and pretty good. I worked my tail off and became the starting wide receiver. I led the entire team in touchdowns as a senior wide receiver for Xaverian and we were conference champions that year, 1995.

Now came by *second* sales position at the young age of eighteen. The *first*, was selling my parents on why they should pay for me to attend a private high school and play football for, quite possibly, the best football program in all of Massachusetts.

I wanted to play football in college at the Division 1 level. Another lofty idea. I had dozens of offers to play at Division 3 and Division 2 colleges. Many, very good schools with excellent football programs. Now, I had to demonstrate my ability and convince (sell) Division 1AA colleges that I could play for them. So we did just that. *We*, meaning my Dad and I, and a local music teacher who had some video production capabilities. We acquired about twenty of my best video clips from playing wide receiver my senior year in high school and created a highlight reel which we sent out to about ten different colleges.

This was the ultimate *sales package* – a highlight video with my best plays sent with a letter inviting myself to play for them… ;)

We landed on Hofstra University in New York, which was transitioning at the time from a Division 3 program to a Division 1AA program so it ended up being a perfect fit. I was invited to camp in the summer of 1991. That year, I was the only player from my high school football team that went on to play on a NCAA Division 1 football program. That was quite a journey, overcoming much adversity, from getting cut from the freshman football team to leading the entire team in touchdowns by my senior year and being the only player to move on to a Division 1 program.

…Of course, skill mattered, but it also took a lot of *selling* along the way.

The only thing I thought about as a kid—from middle school to high school and on to college—was football. I guess you could say it became an obsession. I was on the Hofstra football team for three years and as I was getting ready to enter my senior year, I tore a tendon in my shoulder that ended it all for me. I had been a projected starter as a wide receiver entering my senior year in college and suddenly it was all over. All I had worked so hard for had come to a fast and unexpected end. I had never really thought much about business or a career after college. But now I had to.

I was always entrepreneurial when I was young. I ran a successful personal-training business that I started around the age of eighteen and built up throughout college. I got certified as a Fitness Trainer (CFT) and then *sold* me and my services to two gyms in the Boston area on allowing me to be there only outside personal trainer in their facility, able to market myself to their members, during the summer months while home from college. The gyms each took 15% of my gross profits earned as a trainer. Good deal. I made a lot of money.

…More *selling* of ideas.

At the time, after my shoulder injury ended my football career, I also led the nationally ranked Hofstra Lacrosse team, as their strength and conditioning coach in 1995. I had to *sell* myself on the unusual idea of allowing a "student" (me) to structure and lead the entire off season weight lifting and conditioning program to Coach John Danowski, the Hofstra Lacrosse coach at the time. Today, at the time of this writing, Coach Danowski is the lacrosse coach at Duke University and one of the top lacrosse coaches in the country.

As is often the case in life and in business, when one keeps *selling* themselves, their value and their worth… when one door closes, another tends to open.

That Cold Night On Long Island That Launched My Sales Career...

Then, on one cold, memorable night on Long Island in September 1995, I was invited to a business meeting at a local Holiday Inn. This was a business opportunity meeting for a start up direct sales company in the telecommunications space, American Communications Network (ACN). The business opportunity potential in telecommunications at this time was huge due to the deregulation of the industry. You may remember the wars between AT&T, MCI and Sprint.

What ACN was offering was a business opportunity as a distributor of their services, not a job as an employee. This was all new to me. The startup investment was $495, and at that time, I had about $500 in the bank. The next day, I had $5 in the bank.

I was all in! This investment was a big deal for a young man in college who didn't have a lot of money. I immediately went out and got to work selling ACN's residential telecommunications service to everybody I knew.

As distributors, we would make a small percentage of each customer's monthly phone bill. It was a great little direct-sales business. We were saving people money and, at the same time, making a little bit of money from each customer. In a relatively short time, I had a couple of hundred dollars in "residual income" coming in every month, all before graduating from college. Today, over twenty years later, ACN is almost a Billion dollar company.

It was a great experience for me, at the young age of twenty, to be able to go out, talk to people, and help them save money on their phone bills. I had some success quickly, and that initial burst, while not a lot of money, helped me build momentum as a sale professional. It didn't take long for me to realize that *selling* is where the most money and the most leverage in business is created...

As graduation from Hofstra University approached in the spring of my senior year, I began looking for work as a full-time sales rep. I poured through the classifieds, went on interviews, and about two months before graduating, I was hired as the main sales rep for the entire Long Island territory for an electronic-hardware company. I had to *sell* me, again, on why they should hire a college kid who's never had a full time sales job.

Here I was, just a twenty-year-old kid, and this company was hiring me as a full-time sales rep right out of college. I got a company car, a salary of $30,000 per year, health benefits, and an expense account. Sweet deal at the time. None of my friends could understand it. They were all out partying and thought I was weird for training and working part time to become a salesman. In fact, I started leaving school early to start training with the company part time, two months before graduation, just so I could be prepared to hit the ground running after graduation.

I worked as an outside sales rep for the electronic-hardware company for one year and did very well. Numbers went up and the company had more sales than ever in my territory. It was a great experience but I soon became interested in a much more lucrative career in stocks and the world of investment banking…

Because of the skills I developed from *selling* myself as a football player, to *selling* myself as a personal trainer, to *selling* myself at becoming the youngest sales rep for the electronic hardware company, I ultimately went on to build a 7-figure business in the financial services industry within two short years, and became my firm's first Million Dollar producer at the age of twenty seven.

What is unique and unusual about my success in sales early on is that it happened during a time when there were basically only a few forms of media: telephone and direct mail. And "in-person" media. That was it. There was no Email, no social media, no online video, no search engines, and no Internet. It was old-school sales, the kind that had worked for almost a century before the Internet came along.

In the brokerage and investment business I was basically given a telephone and a stack of Dun & Bradstreet leads, and I was told to call business owners. If I was lucky, they'd send out a brochure for me. That was it. We had to make two hundred to three hundred dials *per day* before we could go home. It was heavy prospecting, and it was exhausting, but it was also <u>exactly</u> what I needed to understand the true meaning of *hard work, speaking* and *selling* – three lost arts today, that we'll dissect together in Sales Velocity...

A New Era...

I spent almost a decade in the financial-services industry and was fortunate enough to catch one of the greatest bull markets of our time. Then everything came crashing down when the dot-com bubble burst. But by that time, I was phasing out of the investment-banking side of the industry and into mortgage banking, where I spent a few more years.

It was in the mortgage banking industry where I got the opportunity to work alongside one of the top sales trainers in the world today, Jordan Belfort. This was obviously <u>after</u> his dark days on Wall Street and <u>before</u> Leonardo DiCaprio put on an Oscar nominated performance playing the role of Jordan Belfort in the movie, *The Wolf Of Wall Street*.

Needless to say, at this time, Jordan had cleaned up his past and was building a legitimate career for himself in the mortgage banking world, where he did quite well. He's a great guy and I learned a lot from him. Today, companies around the world use his Straight Line Persuasion sales training system, the one I trained under before it was even a product.

By 2005, however, I was burned out. The politics and conflicts of interest within the financial- services industry had worn me down and I'd lost interest. What I realized was that I wanted more: more freedom, more control, more from life than working around the clock. I still wanted to make a lot of money, but I wanted to be able to travel and do other things that I hadn't been able to do before.

At some point—I'm not sure when and where—I'd gotten it into my head that I wanted to have an online business, a virtual business, that I could operate from anywhere in the world. This was before Google was a search engine, before Facebook even existed.

Can you imagine *this* world?

It was a cutting-edge concept at the time, even though it's more common than ever today. So I started digging into Internet marketing and information marketing—specifically, how to create, market, and sell products online. I saw very few people selling information online at this time, but I wanted in. I wanted to somehow combine my ten years of traditional, *old-school* sales experience with the *new-school* tools of Internet.

I was on *another* mission...

I immersed myself into the very best Internet Marketing training that existed at the time. Highly expensive, but highly effective, I landed on a group called the Internet Marketing Center. I got schooled on some deep, foreign concepts at the time, such as finding an audience, writing sales letters, lead generation, generating traffic, online PR, creating and selling a product, setting up a merchant account, and setting up e-mail follow-up campaigns. By the time I was through, I was light years ahead of most entrepreneurs, who were barely even using e-mail at the time.

I went from not knowing a thing about the Internet to actually creating a $37 ebook and making regular, around-the-clock, <u>automated</u> sales online — *without* the need to personally make the sales. This was the leverage I was after. And this is the type of leverage I'll talk more about in Sales Velocity…

Later that year, with this newfound Internet Marketing and Online Sales knowledge, I linked up with another direct sales company in the financial education space. A team I was part of built a sophisticated online sales funnel for this company, which successfully blended online sales and marketing with offline live events. It was a huge success. In less than three years, I did well over 7-figures in sales and quickly became the company's top-earning sales consultant, thanks to my deep background and experience in the offline selling world <u>and</u> in the online selling world.

Old School *Selling* Meets New School *Selling*...

I made me first Million in sales before the age of twenty-seven <u>without</u> the Internet. I made my next Million in sales before the age of thirty-five <u>with</u> the Internet. Today, I'm a recognized sales strategist, author and speaker. I share my story with you here, in greater detail than I'm sure most would, not to brag or to impress you, but to impress upon you that experience-based, long-term track records matter today, a lot. More so now than ever, as there is an ever-expanding group of sales, marketing and success "coaches" out there who haven't sold much of anything and aren't very successful.

Odd, I know. Out of integrity, for sure.

Long-term, as in *pre-Internet selling* and *post-Internet selling* track records. Both. Not one or the other. Very few sales trainers, producers and thought leaders in the sales space nowadays have experience and results with both, like I do. I know from first-hand experience, that if you combine traditional (old school) sales methods with modern (new school) online sales methods, it's a very powerful, winning combination - one that very few business owners, to this day, have any idea how to exploit.

This brings us to where we meet today, inside the pages of Sales Velocity where *old school selling* meets *new school selling*, and where you'll have the chance to adopt this proven 3-step formula to transform your business, accelerate your profits, and build real wealth from your business.

Let's begin…

Andrew J. Cass
Miami, Florida 2016
www.AndrewJCass.com

Chapter 1

Why Velocity Is More Important Than Speed...

"Success is not a destination, it's a journey."
– ZIG ZIGLAR

If you had the choice of owning a business that moved very fast in a very <u>clear</u>, certain direction, or being one that expended its efforts along multiple paths, which would you choose?

You can certainly have speed in your business, but without a clear sense of direction, that energy is scattered and unfocused, going off on a million different paths. What's the point then, of so much effort if it's not going toward a specific goal? Unfortunately, this is becoming a much more common problem in today's overwhelmed, distracted, always-connected world. It's a constant struggle to keep up with your business while, at the same time, reaching out through dozens of communications networks in the hope that some of the people you reach will become potential customers.

As people continue to move in an increasingly wider range of directions in terms of what they read, whom they listen to, what they watch, and how they communicate, businesses often find themselves in *reactive* mode. What these speed-driven entrepreneurs don't understand is that you can't be a jack-of-all-trades and be effective. A jack-of-all-trades is a master of none. Along with speed, you need to seek *velocity.*

By definition, you can have speed without velocity, but not velocity without speed. Velocity is speed in a very certain, clear direction, and having velocity in your sales process is how you achieve real wealth in your business.

You're essentially taking all of that scattered energy and focusing it on one, systems-driven process, one that is specific for your business and encompasses a clearly defined system for *marketing,* a clearly defined system for *selling,* and a clearly defined system for customer development, or *follow-up.* And *that* is the Sales Velocity philosophy...

How To Build Real Wealth Inside Your Business...

The richest company in the world is Apple. Their business model is one of the best examples of a clear systems-driven, process-oriented business. Apple has a set system in place for everything: marketing, selling, and follow-up.

But as diverse as Apple may seem when it comes to its hold on the market, it has a very clear focus. By *Wikipedia's* definition, the company is "an American multinational technology company that designs, develops, and sells consumer electronics, computer software, and online services."[1]

---

[1]   "Apple, Inc.," Wikipedia, **https://en.wikipedia.org/wiki/Apple_Inc**.

By specializing in these specific areas, Apple has created a very definite and known niche for itself in today's market. And that's exactly what it takes. In a market oversaturated with general businesses trying to be something for everyone, it's the specialists that stand out.

This reminds of something the late, great Zig Ziglar said: *"Don't be a wandering generality. Be a meaningful specific."*

In the world of small-to-medium businesses, a specialist can be defined as the highest-paid entrepreneur on the income ladder. Doctors, for instance, are specialists in their specific fields. Professional athletes are specialists because they play a certain sport and hold a specific position within that sport. Even experts in business become specialists when they consult on a specific industry or author a book on a specific topic. They focus on a <u>clear</u> and certain niche.

When you narrow your focus in this manner, you become noticeable. For example, you aren't an attorney; you're a family law attorney. You aren't a photographer; you're a food portrait photographer. You aren't a surgeon; you're a heart surgeon. People looking for your specific service are much more likely to find you because you stand out as doing or having *exactly* what they need. Specializing allows you to gain traction with your ideal clientele, and once you have traction, you can start gaining momentum. And momentum inevitably leads to growth.

Ultimately, you want to get your business to a point where it creates the lifestyle you want. It doesn't just make some money; it creates the kind of *leverage* and *freedom* that allows you to convert income into wealth so that you can go off and do other things you want to do, such as play golf, vacation, or whatever else you've always dreamed of doing. Most business owners never get there. They end up going into business and, basically, starting an expensive job.

When your business is efficiently organized with <u>clearly</u> defined systems set in place, it creates leverage and freedom for you, the owner. For most of us, the ultimate goal of money is not to have the physical cash but, rather, to have what that money will buy. It's a means to an end. You can make money, but if you're working twelve hours a day, you're not enjoying it; you don't have real wealth…

When you're a wealthy business owner, you can live life on your terms. You can go out for a nice dinner anytime, take that trip to Tahiti, indulge in your hobbies, or buy nice clothes. Wealth allows you to not only have, but to also *sustain* all the things that you want in life.

But if your business is floundering and there are no sales systems and processes in place to help you reach the point of wealth, then you'll never have that ideal lifestyle. You need to systematize your business—make it work for you instead of you working for it, so that you can free up more time and work less yet, get the same results. That's the key.

So few businesses actually take the time to really strategize and create sales and marketing systems, but those that do are remarkably successful. When everything and everyone is accountable, when it's <u>clear</u> exactly what needs to be done and the whole system is moving in a well-defined direction, that's when you have *velocity*. And when you have velocity, you have the ability to turn that <u>clearly</u> focused energy into *real wealth*.

Old School Versus New School Selling...

Coming into the sales arena when I did, in the mid-1990s, has provided me with a very unique perspective and range of experience, as I detailed in the introduction of this book. I've been able to blend the skills learned both before and after the Internet boom—the real human connection that we had to have before today's means of instant communication, along with current technology.

Where many salespeople have experience in one school or the other, very few have done both and adapted to both. Old-school sales professionals, for instance, still haven't really harnessed the Internet. It's a fear of the unknown that goes both ways because new-school salespeople wouldn't be caught dead sitting down face-to-face with someone or cold calling someone out of the blue. They wouldn't do it! On the other hand, I have no fear of either. I can sell on the phone, in person, in front of a room, on a webinar, and on video. I've done it all.

In failing to focus on both schools, old and new, you're failing to maximize your selling potential. If you're selling and communicating in the old-school format, you have a great presence on the phone, in person or on stage, but you're not blending that with the tools that we live by today, such as social media, online video, webinars, e-mail follow-up, and SMS text, etc. you're missing out. And vice versa! By not blending the two, you're leaving whole forms of communication, whole forms of interaction, on the table.

It's not one or the other today. It's "both." I've found that top performing entrepreneurs and business owners have a "both" mentality.

The Perfect Sales Process...

Who wouldn't want the perfect sales process for their business, right?

After twenty years in the sales and marketing world, I've found that the perfect sales process consists of three steps, not five, not ten—just three. And when these three are in place, in a very specific and <u>clear</u> order—in alignment—*selling more with less resistance* becomes a reality.

Here's a breakdown and a glimpse at the three parts of Sales Velocity:

Step #1: Direct Response Marketing

Before any real selling can take place, you must lead with direct response marketing. Better known as lead generation, direct response marketing is what ultimately brings your ideal customers to you instead of you having to expend unnecessary energy *chasing* after them. You need to pique the interest of your ideal customers, inform them, and educate them <u>first</u>. When you try to sell first, without informing, educating and providing value <u>first</u>, you're more likely to fail. And you're wasting time and energy that could be put to much better and more productive use.

Direct response marketing can be done in the form of free reports, videos, webinars and any other form of multimedia that either *solves* a problem for your potential clients or shows them how to *avoid* one. It is designed to educate first, sell second. Otherwise known as, "Education Based Marketing." This is key. This is the foundation.

Hunters chase. Fishermen lure. Which are you? More on that later...

Step #2: Multimedia Selling

Once your prospects have been warmed up with the information they need on how to solve their specific problems, or how to avoid them, *then* you can make a sales presentation. If you try to sell first, as most salespeople try to do, you could easily wind up scaring off a potential customer. This creates *resistance*. Multimedia selling simply means using multiple forms of *media* to deliver your presentation—video, webinar, sales letter, in person, direct mail, e-mail, on the phone, or any other form of communication—because everyone has different preferences when it comes to consuming information.

Having your sales presentation and your conversations with prospects structured in *multiple* forms of *media* means you'll get more people to consume your message in the way *they* prefer. This multimedia approach is <u>critical</u> because it's a battle to *get* and *keep* attention today. At the same time, multimedia is equally as important in your follow-up because most prospects will not buy right away. A strategic multimedia follow-up process is very impressive to your prospects. Yet, so few do it, if at all, even with the advanced technology that automates much of it. Employing multiple forms of media to get your message across is your greatest opportunity to shine above and beyond the competition.

Step #3: Customer Experience

Customer experience, a.k.a. customer service, is a *lost art.* You may be asking, *"How is customer service part of the selling process? Doesn't that come after the sale is made?"*

The truth is, it's very much a part of the sales process—that is, unless you'd rather your new customer or client forget about you after the first sale, to never buy from you again, and never refer prospects to you. Think about it. How many businesses will you *not* buy from again because their customer service and your experience with them was terrible or nonexistent? Now think about the businesses you continue to buy from because of the excellent customer service you've received. How much more business did you give the company that treated you well as opposed to the one that never cared to follow up with you after the first sale?

Most companies are too focused on bringing in new customers and not servicing their existing ones. The result of this small thinking is little repeat business, low customer value, weak profits, and very few referrals. Not a pretty picture after all the work that was done to get the customer in the first place, right?

The great majority of small-business owners and entrepreneurs today begin with Step #2. You've seen it, when the first thing salespeople do is launch right into a "pitch" about how great their products and services are. Then they chase their prospective clients around for weeks to get an answer, which creates immediate *resistance.* Ultimately, they annoy their prospects, frustrate themselves, and rarely make the sale.

However, when **Direct Response Marketing** precedes a sound **Multimedia Selling** process and an impressive **Customer Experience** follows that, you have the makings of a perfect sales process in your business. There is no greater asset. The best part is that your prospects will often feel as if they *bought* from you rather than feeling *sold* by you. Big difference!

This book will show you how to do exactly this: *attract* business instead of *chasing* it, and slow down the sales process so that you not only make more sales but gain <u>customers for life.</u>

Part 1:
Direct Response Marketing

Chapter 2

How To Go from *Hunter* to *Fisherman*...

"Get out there and sell something, will ya?
America needs the business!"
– ZIG ZIGLAR

The more quickly a business can become *marketing-driven* instead of just *sales-driven*, the more sustainable it becomes. Most businesses today launch right into "selling, selling, selling," getting more salespeople in the field and just selling as much as possible. But the truth is, no one likes to be sold. However, everyone loves to buy. Ponder that.

Without a good, strategic, thought-based marketing plan in place that warms up your ideal audience beforehand, you're going to meet a lot of *resistance* on the sales end. That's where a solid direct response marketing strategy becomes invaluable to the success of your business. It's the "on ramp", so to speak...

Direct response marketing means speaking to a very specific and direct audience as opposed to broader marketing, which tries to cast a wide net over a broad pool of people in the hopes that at least a few of the people reached will become prospective customers. It is, in essence, *targeted, niche-based marketing*.

When you engage in direct response marketing, you *know* who your audience is, you know your niche, and you have some basic demographics for an ideal client in mind: older, younger; male, female; white collar, blue collar. Once you have that in mind, once you've defined your niche and niche market, you can begin directly marketing to those people, getting them to come to you instead of the other way around.

Most business owners today *hunt* or chase after their prospects. Very few take the time to work out a system that *lures* the ideal customer to them. By using the fisherman approach as opposed to hunting your prospects, you face far less *resistance* because you're essentially putting the right information (a.k.a. bait) out there making it much easier for potential customers to come looking for you.

With targeted direct response marketing, you're educating your prospects and exchanging value with them by providing information either physically or online. Then, instead of taking a weird, awkward first step right into the sales process, the sale simply becomes an obvious next step.

If I were to make the decision today that I wanted to go out and fish for blue marlin, for example, I know that I would need to first find out what bait and lures are specific to that fish's interests and appetite. I would also need to know where to look; I wouldn't go fishing in a duck pond, for instance, or a salt-water creek. Once I have that information, I can go directly after blue marlin.

But if I wing it and say, *"I'm going fishing today,"* and just throw a worm in the water, hoping for the best, then not much is going to happen. And even if I were to catch a fish, it very likely wouldn't be a blue marlin. Get it?

The same thing happens in business. If I don't take the time to identify an audience and find out what they're attracted to, what their pain points and needs are, and how my products or services can be the solution to their problems, then I can't fish for them. I can't put any information or education or any type of free material out in the marketplace that directly addresses my ideal clients. Instead, I'm just throwing that worm out or casting a wide net into the water, hoping for the best.

Hope is not a strategy.

Unfortunately, that jack-of-all-trades-and-master-of-none approach winds up costing business owners a whole lot of time, wasted energy and <u>money</u>... with very little positive results.

But the vast majority of businesses are doing exactly that every day: they're casting their nets, using whatever bait is on hand and fishing anywhere and everywhere they can, winging it and hoping for the best. And that's if they're marketing at all!

Others just scrap the whole marketing process and launch directly into the sales pitch, which more than likely ends up making both them and their prospects feel awkward. Even worse, they end up chasing those prospects to get a decision. They *hunt* them down until they themselves lose all of their authority and position in the marketplace. Even though a lot of salespeople think of this as follow-up (which we discuss more in Part 3), let me tell you that this kind of approach is exactly the opposite.

Is it any wonder why so many businesses fail so fast?

What you want to do, right from the start, is move as far away from being a *dumb hunter* and as close to being a *savvy fisherman* as possible…

Chapter 3
Niching Down...

"You don't "pay the price" for success –
you enjoy the benefits of success."
– ZIG ZIGLAR

When you're a specialist to a certain audience, you become far more relevant to that audience. As the saying goes, there are: "riches in niches." Take a heart surgeon for instance…. Heart surgeons do heart surgery only. They don't do a shoulder surgery on Tuesday and a knee surgery on Thursday. Instead, people fly in from all over the world to see heart surgeons because they specialize in such an important part of the body.

As a business owner, you need to BE that heart surgeon, per say. You have to think about where you want to specialize and how you can make it completely clear that you're the go-to expert in your space. In doing this, you will eliminate a lot of selling resistance. Specializing also creates price elasticity because potential customers will rarely chop you down in price if you're a specialist. Being a recognized specialist as opposed to an unrecognized generalist makes you much more desirable and, in their minds, worth the investment.

So how do you become a specialist? How do you niche down?

By taking a good, hard look at your business and determining what makes YOU unique. What is your unique skill set, strength, or talent? Once you have that unique quality, you can start to shape your business model around it. That remarkable characteristic becomes your Unique Selling Proposition, or USP, which makes you and your business attractive to your audience.

This is especially relevant today as we have more choices and options out there than ever before. In fact, there's great risk in remaining a generalist and not moving into a specialized area. That wasn't the case ten years ago, before the Internet became such an integral part of everyone's lives, but today there are so many options that people don't have the time or patience for a generalist. They want and need someone who can take care of their <u>specific need</u> and can do it quickly with a quality result (This is especially what affluent buyers want).

This trending preference for specialists over generalists is a paradigm shift in business that should be a wake-up call to any business owners who feel their business is becoming stale and stagnant, that they're just not making the kind of sales they should be, or did in the past. If this is the case for you, there's a good chance your business is being viewed, as Zig Ziglar says, as a "wandering generality. Which means it's time to move up the income ladder to become a "meaningful specific" by creating, or redefining, *your* Unique Selling Proposition...

Chapter 4
What's Your USP?

"Don't become a wandering generality.
Be a meaningful specific."
– ZIG ZIGLAR

Several decades ago, Domino's Pizza was just a regular pizza operation until founder Tom Monaghan began offering the famous thirty-minute delivery guarantee in the early 1970s. This feature became incredibly popular and pushed the growing chain from being just another pizza operation to becoming a *specialty* pizza delivery company. Domino's was no longer in the pizza business; it was in the pizza-delivery business.

Here is the Unique Selling Proposition they created which exploded the company's growth. You may remember this:

"Fresh, hot pizza delivered in
30-minutes or less. Guaranteed."

This is a textbook USP. As in, *perfect*. This out-of-the-box approach was Domino's Unique Selling Proposition and it was one of the key factors that fueled the company's launch into becoming a multi-billion dollar, publicly traded franchise.

Your USP is invaluable. It should be the core of your business and the central philosophy on which you base all of your business decisions. It should be your identity and what people recognize about you, first and foremost.

The mistake a lot of business owners make is that they spend too much time on branding, cosmetics, logos, and looking good in general, and not enough time on developing and promoting their USP.

Big mistake. USP must come first, all else comes second. Don't let anyone tell you different.

Last I checked, we're all in business to sell things, not to look good, right? This is not *Glamour* Magazine. This is a "for-profit" business, right? If your focus has been on finding just the right font size for your mailers or modifying your website colors and logos for the umpteenth time, then you need to stop. Stop looking at the surface issues and start looking at your real position in the marketplace.

The late, great John Rohn, author of *The Art of Exceptional Living*, once said, "*Most people major in minor things.*" Don't be one of them. Instead, start carving out your unique and valuable position in the marketplace.

Inside my Sales Velocity Inner Circle, our Unique Selling Proposition at the time of this writing, is: "*Advanced Sales Training For Professional Entrepreneurs & Business Owners.*" As you can see, it's very specific. Clear. Not simple solutions, but "Advanced" solutions. Not for wanna-be entrepreneurs or business owners, but for "Professionals."

[To take a tour inside Sales Velocity Inner Circle, visit:
www.SalesVelocityInnerCircle.com]

This is what you're after with your USP – <u>clear</u>, precise language that *attracts* the right audience, not deters them or confuses them, like the majority of businesses do today, unfortunately.

In fact, you'd be well served to just look at what almost everyone else in your market is doing and start doing the opposite! The "mediocre majority" is often wrong and rarely noticed.

A great example of going against the grain and becoming "unique" is Cronuts. While everyone else was making plain old donuts, they showed up on the scene with a croissant-doughnut pastry that's made by laminating dough in grape seed oil. The fried pastry is then sugared, filled and glazed. It's become a worldwide phenomenon. All because they took the plain and ordinary and made it different and *unique,* and unique to them by trademarking the entire process. Very cool.

When you stand out in the sea of sameness, that's when you start attracting a lot of greatness to your business. It all begins with finding <u>your</u> Unique Selling Proposition. This is at the foundation of the very best business models in the world. And it's the starting point of Sales Velocity...

When I work directly with private clients, it is this "unique" angle I'm always looking for, this "contrarian" approach. And I often find it. And when I do, they become way more interesting and relevant to a select, niche audience. They move from *hunter* to *fisherman*…

Chapter 5
Trusting The Bait...

"The fastest way to success is to replace bad habits with good habits."
- ZIG ZIGLAR

Doing your research, finding the right spot, and using the right bait are all integral to a good marketing strategy, but even if you've done everything in the world to hook the right fish, they still aren't going to bite if they don't trust your bait. This is where the value of strategic positioning comes in.

Just as experienced fishermen know how to twitch the line exactly to mimic the bait on the end, strategic positioning in your ideal marketplace helps you gain the trust of your prospects. And that's where the value of education and information-based marketing comes in.

By educating your audience through as many multimedia mechanisms as possible—from in-person or online training to content, video, discovery days, free trials and so on, you're building familiarity and tearing down a lot of initial *resistance*. And as your prospects warm to you and receive this beneficial education and information with no strings attached, you become valuable to them. You create value, educate your audience, give things away or sell them inexpensive, and basically, allow them into your world, inviting them to learn more about what you do. Once they're interested, *then and only then* can you move into Part 2: Multimedia Selling.

Remember, most begin here, selling right away. And this is met with a lot of *resistance.* It's too soon. The Sales Velocity formula moves here second, not first. A huge difference.

Now that you get the importance of creating a Direct Response Marketing foundation, lets go to Part 2…

Part 2:
Multimedia Selling

Chapter 6

You *Might* Have It All Backwards...

"It's not what happens to you that matters. It's how you respond to what happens to you that makes a difference."
– ZIG ZIGLAR

If you're starting the sales process here—with actually selling—you've got it all wrong. Most business owners start with selling, putting a bunch of salespeople on the phone, and chasing prospects. It's difficult to build trust that way. Potential clients don't think, *"You know, I'm really starting to trust that guy who's called me seven times in the last fifteen hours. I think I'll buy from him."*

Chasing prospects like that is not just hunting them but hunting them by driving into the woods on an ATV in the hopes of tracking down a deer. You've not only scared them off but they'll probably never return to that part of the woods!

But when a gracefully lured prospect gets a FedEx package with an information kit, a couple of e-mails from the company providing them with helpful resources, and a courtesy phone call or two about a free, upcoming webinar, then there's a much greater likelihood that they'll take the time to learn more about you. And be impressed by you.

All of these little things—these little bits of helpful information delivered using technology, media, automation, or other creative means—help your prospects learn about you on their own time and by their own will. They don't feel sold to; they feel as if they've made the decision to learn more on their own. And if they *do* decide to go with you, they'll feel as if they've made that decision on their own.

Remember what I said earlier, *"people hate to be sold, but they love to buy."*

What's more, whether they realize it or not, prospects tend to be impressed when they see a true multimedia selling campaign in action. To your prospective customers or clients, this makes your company appear well organized and thorough because they're receiving things such as a package in the mail or a free gift or an invitation to a webinar in a timely manner.

These detailed and well-thought-out presentations are impressive because they're consistent, and when you make the effort to ensure everything matches from a branding standpoint, that everything is congruent, and that multiple forms of media are being used, then you come across as having your finger on the pulse of your niche marketplace; you're perceived by your prospect, either consciously or subconsciously, as a professional. More important, congruency and consistency create *trust*. And trust is the gold key in selling. Bar none.

Whenever a prospect signs up for one of my Sales Velocity online workshops or live training events, we call them beforehand to remind them about the event, they get emails and text message reminders, and afterward, they get a letter and a gift for attending. And if they decide to become members, we always over deliver on training content and value. The result is that most people who attend and become members see all of these things happening and think, *"Wow, they really have their act together. They must care. I can trust them."*

Most businesses, however, are too lazy or narrow-minded to put all of these pivot points in place. Novice business owners often just use e-mail because it's free, even though it's one of the least recognized forms of media in existence because of the sheer volume we receive on a daily basis. When it comes to *attracting* your ideal customers, multimedia is key.

Chapter 7
The Lost Art...

"You don't drown by falling in water,
you only drown if you stay there."
– ZIG ZIGLAR

When people tell me I'm good at sales, and I tell them I'm really not, this often comes as quite a surprise from a 20-year sales veteran and the author of a book on *sales*. My response is simple: *"I'm really not a great sales person but I am pretty good at communicating."*

A quality communicator will <u>always</u> close more sales, always win more cases in a courtroom, always get elected to office, and always win over the opposite sex. You get the point.

Most salespeople incorrectly focus *only* on achieving better sales skills and not on becoming better communicators. Again, it's "both." You can take all the courses you want on improving sales, but in the end, it's how you communicate the concepts you've learned that makes them effective. Learning how to communicate well creates confidence. And the more confidence you have, the more confidence your prospect will have *in you*. And <u>this</u> is the key to selling today.

At the same time, good communicators are also more believable and trustworthy because they aren't just speaking well; they're listening too. To dust off an old cliché, communication is a two-way street. If you can do both—speak well and listen well—you'll really begin to tear down a lot of those selling-resistance walls and, in the end, you'll work less for greater rewards.

Finally, to sell well, you need to believe in your product. The best salespeople out there have an unshakable belief in what they sell, and it comes out. They're passionate about what they're selling. What's more, passion breeds confidence, so when you combine that pride in your product, that passion, with excellent communication skills, your confidence and selling ability know no bounds.

In fact, you stop selling in the sense that most people think about selling. Instead, when you believe wholeheartedly in what you sell, when you're excited and enthusiastic about it and communicate that well, the people around you naturally become more attracted to whatever product or service has lit this fire in you. You're no longer pitching; you're sharing, building a relationship and igniting in others that spark of excitement, that desire to find out more.

Inside my Sales Velocity Inner Circle membership, one of the key trainings I lead is a live *Mental Toughness Sales Training Call* series where I dig deep into these concepts of mastering communication and becoming a more persuasive, influential professional, which all leads to more control, and more profit!

[For more info, visit: **www.SalesVelocityInnerCircle.com**]

Chapter 8
The Secret Behind The Highest Sales Conversions...

"Yesterday ended last night. Today is a brand new day and it's yours!"
– ZIG ZIGLAR

This might be the most important chapter in the entire book. What you're going to find here is a big secret behind the best sales processes in the world. Read closely...

Passion is one thing when you're selling in person, but the fact is, if you're going to labor over every single sale, you're going to burn out quickly. How then, can you <u>consistently</u> sell without putting as much of that focused time into *personally* making every single sale? How do you make multimedia work for you?

Media such as video, webinar presentations, and direct mail can be invaluable in doing a lot of the sifting and sorting for you, dividing the valuable potential customers from the browsers. Or as I like to say: separating *suspects* from *prospects*. But to reach as many of those prospects as possible, you need to truly embrace all of these multimedia approaches, simultaneously...

Why?

Because everyone takes in, consumes and absorbs information differently nowadays. Very few consider this when crafting a sales process or a sales funnel. And many miss a ton of sales as a result.

Read that again.

You may have narrowed down your niche demographic to a specific industry, age, education level, and even gender, but what you can't narrow down is how people *consume* information. And "consumption" is the key today because now, more than ever, we have information and offers flying at us from all angles. This isn't about to change any time soon. So, getting your prospect to pay attention and take in the necessary information is a battle today.

This is why the Sales Velocity system is so <u>critical</u> for you to integrate all three parts into your business model – because it gets "attention" (that's the Direct Response Marketing piece) and it forces "consumption" (this is the Multi-Media Selling piece).

Let's dive into this *consumption* piece...

There are essentially three ways in which people consume info:

1. Audio (sound)

2. Visual (sight)

3. Kinesthetic (movement)

Some absorb information in just one of these three ways. Others absorb information in two of the three ways. Rarely do you see people who prefer to consume information through all three methods though. But no matter the many ways in which your prospects absorb information, each of these methods will only achieve a certain response from a certain number of prospects.

So why not integrate them ALL into *your* sales presentations to crank up your sales conversions?

Think about that. Today, it's more achievable to make this happen than <u>ever before</u> with technology and automation. Yet, surprisingly, so few have multimedia sales processes and sales funnels...

This is the big *secret* behind some of the best business models in the world. They are masters at integrating audio, visual and kinesthetic modalities throughout their sales presentations so that the maximum number of people plug in, <u>consume</u> and <u>absorb</u>. More importantly, they take action!

This is why webinars and video sales letters have been so successful over the past few years, selling products and services to the tune of Billions. There is an audio, visual *and* kinesthetic component. The viewer can see, hear and there is movement. This is the best of all worlds. And it's very hypnotic.

Over the past five years or so I've literally sold Millions of dollars worth of products and services by webinar and webcast presentations. And the best part is, you can be in front of hundreds, even thousands, at one time, from the comfort of your home or office. Plus, it can be recorded, automated and can run for you 24 hours a day, 7 days a week just like a TV commercial!

If you're not somehow integrating all three methods of consumption into your sales process, you're probably failing to reach a lot of prospects that might otherwise have decided to buy your product *if* you'd presented it to them in the way in which *they* are wired to absorb it.

For instance, if I were a financial advisor (which I used to be many years ago) and if I was only selling to people by telephone (audio), I'd be leaving out two other consumption methods. I'd also be ignoring one of the best *sales assistants* in existence: the Internet! Of course, it's perfectly fine to present and sell by telephone and/or arrange in-person appointments, but with technology such as e-mail marketing, video and webinar marketing, social media, and so on, you can get a far bigger reach and be far more efficient.

A phone call can still be a key piece of the puzzle, and should be, but let's take a look at how to maximize its effectiveness...

I love the good, old fashion telephone in a sales process. As mentioned in the introduction, I came up in sales at the tender age of twenty-two when there was no Internet and no Email. As a young stockbroker and investment banker during the pre-Internet days, I had to learn telephone communication skills backwards and forward. It was all we had to make a sales presentation back then. All we had for *technology* was the phone and direct mail. That was it. Those were the "big two" in those days.

Today, the telephone, as part of an overall multimedia sales process is very effective. I say it's essential. Whenever I am utilizing the phone in my own sales process or sales funnels or that of a client, I stack the deck in our favor <u>prior</u> to any telephone (or in-person) presentation. For example, ideally, I will usually send a series of Emails with content, videos, and/or success stories or case studies <u>prior</u> to the call. Plus, even better, a Direct Mail package sent with the same info or a book, report, or CD, etc. is amazing for building credibility and trust <u>prior</u> to a telephone call or presentation.

Very few take these extra steps <u>prior</u> to a telephone or in-person presentation. Many face a lot of *resistance* as a result...

One of my private clients, John Rizvi, is a successful patent attorney and an incredibly sharp marketer. Before any of his prospects come to his office to meet him and learn about his trademark or patent work, he mails them a FedEx package along with a DVD presentation so that they have all the information they need <u>prior</u> to their first appointment with him. No appointments happen until this is received first. This helps John because he doesn't have to launch into a lengthy, "here's-how-things-work" speech. It also positions John much better, as a clear expert, who took the time to send a package. This builds trust. It also means his prospects (once *cold*, now *warm*) are inclined to move forward and buy because they've received priority information by mail, may have watched the presentation, and still chose to come in or book a telephone appointment. Because of this, he doesn't have to do a whole lot of heavy lifting when it comes to making a sale. In other words, he *sells more with less resistance.*

My Sales Velocity brand is another example of leaving no stone unturned when it comes to multimedia. Frankly, we're a multimedia machine, leaving no form of media untouched. I, literally, wake up every day, every week, and ask myself:

"How do we integrate every form of media possible to promote our advanced sales training and reach as many people as possible?"

The Sales Velocity Approach To Multimedia Selling: Omnipresence

Dan Kennedy taught be this term, "omnipresence." It means you and your business are, essentially, <u>everywhere</u>, in all forms of *media*. This not only puts you front-of-mind, it also demonstrates consistency and congruency in the marketplace, which all leads to <u>trust</u>. And creating trust, as you know, is the key to selling success…

Here's how I do it under my Sales Velocity business model:

Live Training: Every month I host a live online workshop (webcast) and periodically throughout the year I put on live, in-person Sales Velocity seminars in which the public can gain access. I also conduct very advanced Mental Toughness Sales Training calls.

Direct Mail: Every month, we publish the *Sales Velocity Insider* print newsletter that goes out to all of our Sales Velocity Inner Circle members. We also send out regular post card reminders about upcoming Sales

Funnel Mastery workshops or Mental Toughness Sales Training Calls.

Email: Every week, I publish the *Sales Velocity Insider* eNewsletter which consists of one insider secret for selling more with less resistance, usually in video.

Telephone: My Sales Velocity Inner Circle membership team makes regular, outgoing phone calls throughout the month to members about upcoming mastermind meetings or events and to new guests who've registered for one of our trainings.

SMS Text: We send out weekly text message alerts to follow up important Email alerts since Email inboxes are cluttered today and many Emails can get missed.

Social Media: We maintain a "public" Sales Velocity Inner Circle Facebook group for anyone to come in, for free, and join the conversation about increasing their sales skills. We also maintain a "private" Facebook group for my Sales Velocity Mastermind Members and VIP Private Clients to be able to communicate with one another, post ideas, and get feedback in between meetings or phone sessions with me. Twitter and YouTube are used as well.

Podcast: I host the Sales Velocity podcast show in iTunes, where I personally lead a sales training or conduct an interview with a hand-picked expert Entrepreneur, Business Owner or Sales Professional.

Video Production: I have a professional video production team for all online and offline trainings and events. Every training that I conduct is available for replay, adds to our training archive, and is used to create information products. And just recently, has been built into our own University.

Information Products: Over the past eight years or so I led a live, in-person business growth seminar in South Florida every month. Initially, in partnership with GKIC Insider's Circle as a Dan Kennedy Certified Business Advisor, and then under the name, Renegade South Florida Entrepreneurs. That's roughly 100 seminars. No small task. We captured the very best of those training events on video, had them professionally produced in HD quality, and built our own, advanced business growth online training platform called Renegade Entrepreneur University.

[For more information about Renegade Entrepreneur University, *where ordinary Business Owners become top earning Entrepreneurs,* visit: **www.MyRenegadeU.com**]

That's a lot, I know. I get tired just writing it. ;)

I also know that very few can keep up and maintain this level of *omnipresence* in the marketplace. As you can see, no "media stone" is left unturned. This is how to lead and dominate…

Bottom line: When you are seen <u>everywhere</u> and you leverage all media, old school <u>and</u> new school, you immediately create *consistency* and congruency because everyone is consistently seeing you and your marketing as reassuringly *congruent*. With those two factors in place, you can begin establishing trust. And at the end of the day in selling, if you're not seeking the highest level of trust, you are creating the greatest amount of unnecessary *resistance* in your sales process. Period.

Chapter 9

We Are All in Sales Today. Get Over It...

"You were designed for accomplishment, engineered for success, and endowed with the seeds of greatness."
– ZIG ZIGLAR

When I was in my very first outside sales job right out of college, I had a cassette tape of the late, great sales trainer Zig Ziglar that I listened to in my car. At the time, he was probably one of the most recognized sales trainers and motivational speakers around. Something he said stuck with me, and is actually quite funny:

"Timid salespeople have skinny kids."

That statement made me realize that all business owners and entrepreneurs need to view themselves as professional salespeople of their products and services because, in the end, the most successful ones are the best promoters of themselves. They're out there in front of their audience, constantly promoting. Whether it's their product, an event, or something big, it's always over-the-top, and that's why they're so successful.

As an entrepreneur or business owner, you are *in* the sales business. Period. A doctor, for instance, is a salesperson of medical services. A lawyer is a salesperson of legal services, etc.

The longer you reject this fact, the more you're resisting success because *nothing happens in business until something is sold.* Payrolls won't get met, employees can't be hired, products can't be developed, and growth and expansion can't happen until your products and services are <u>sold</u> on a regular basis.

Promotion isn't a bad thing. It's only viewed that way by people who simply aren't comfortable with themselves and don't have enough belief in what it is they are selling. Plain and simple. Promotion in and of itself is just selling an idea, a philosophy, a concept. And the ones who don't promote—well, they may not have skinny kids, but they certainly have skinny bank accounts.

At the end of the day, people buy from people, not from nameless, faceless companies. When a strong, charismatic person is the face of a company, people are more inclined to buy from them because they feel that personal connection. Think, Steve Jobs. Take Richard Branson with the Virgin brand, or Donald Trump with the Trump brand, or marketing legends such as Dan Kennedy or Jay Abraham. I serve as that strong personality with a twenty-year sales background and track record, leading my Sales Velocity brand in videos and other promotional materials.

It would be difficult for a company to just run on the brand without the personality associated with the brand. To have less resistance when you sell, it's smart to have a personality that connects with the outside. Otherwise, it's just boring and dull, and it makes selling much more difficult.

How much of YOU or a big personality is front and center in your business?

…Food for thought.

Bottom line: The faster you make your sales process and the selling of your product or service THE focal point of your business, the better off you'll be, the happier you'll be, the more liberated you'll be and the more leverage you'll create. And leverage is the name of the game.

The longer you fight this fact, the more resistance you'll face every day as you try to attract customers and clients. And you'll wind up having to do all kinds of things you may not want to do. And there's a real chance that your business could turn very little, if any, profit…

And one of the most essential parts of that mind-set *shift* is understanding that a new customer is far more valuable than just making a sale. Which leads us directly to Part 3, the Customer Experience…

Part 3:
Customer Experience

Chapter 10
Does Your Business Have A Sales Prevention Department?

"There is no elevator to success, you have to take the stairs."
– ZIG ZIGLAR

I've never forgotten this one question I heard asked by Dan Kennedy years back:

"Is it better to get a customer to make a sale? Or is it better to make a sale to get a customer?"

Think about it.

Hopefully it's obvious to you that the better scenario is the latter not the former. As in, once a sale is made it then becomes time to <u>develop</u> a customer relationship…

I can tell your first-hand having worked with hundreds of business owners and entrepreneurs, that 95% of them believe the correct answer is the former, the first part of the question. As a result, 95% struggle to get and keep customers. Part 3 of Sales Velocity will show how to be part of the *other* 5%.

Customer development is the key to building real wealth in your business. Let's talk about it…

The Problem...

Most business owners literally prevent sales daily and they don't even realize it. They have such poor processes in place that when prospects are ready to make a decision, the process is so unprofessional and unplanned it creates a disconnect that can, quite literally, drive customers away because they're so annoyed and frustrated.

Ever been there? Of course you have! How many times have you said: *"I'll never do business with them again!"*

As the saying goes, *"you never get a second chance to make a first impression."* And this is truer than ever in business. Most don't consider this...

If a prospect is ready to make a decision and you don't have a solid, elegant sales process in place, if you're just winging it (like 95% do), then you're going to lose A LOT of business. Because you will not get a second chance to *impress*. Not today. There are far too many options beside you. You need to be sharp-as-a-tack today from front to back (all 3 parts of Sales Velocity formula).

Sales prevention can happen during the sale, but it actually hurts the business owner even more when a poor or nonexistent follow-up process prevents *future* sales – The topic of Part 3.

Unfortunately, the follow-up process is when a lot of these *sales prevention departments* kick in. I know that term is humorous, and I often do have fun with it in my sales trainings and seminars, but when you don't follow up properly, or at all, you lose the opportunity of turning that one sale into recurring sales and/or referral opportunities. And *that* is a BIG "double loss."

Future sales from <u>existing customers</u> are where the greatest customer value growth occurs because it transforms a "one-and-done" customer into a valuable, recurring and referring customer. Big difference. And *this* is your core necessity for building real wealth in your business…

Chapter 11
You Just Got A Customer, Now What?

"For every sale you miss because you're too enthusiastic, you'll miss a hundred because you're not enthusiastic enough."
– ZIG ZIGLAR

If you're in that 95% category I mentioned in the previous chapter, like most businesses, after you get a customer, nothing happens. Literally. You've made the sale, and it's on with life, on to the next new customer. And that's the problem. Hopefully, you're not like most, but if you are and you're struggling with your sales, or you're struggling for referrals or for additional sales from existing customers, it's likely that your customer follow-up program is either suffering or nonexistent.

The greatest opportunity to make additional sales—easier sales—and to increase customer value is when you get new customers to buy for the first time. They've finally made a decision, and they've exchanged money, and in that moment, they're most receptive to whatever else you can do to increase the quality of your relationship with them. But so few business owners do anything more during that <u>critical</u> time frame, apart from delivering the product or service.

It's as if they're saying, *"I don't want more money from that customer. I'm perfectly rich right now and I don't want referrals because I have all the customers I could ever want."* It's as big a risk as it is a bad decision.

So what can you do to *"wow"* them during that vital receptive period? How can you proactively encourage the next vital step by creating an *experience* that will encourage your new customer to not only spend more money with you but also refer other new customers to you?

That's the Million Dollar question...

Chapter 12
The Morning After...

"Failure is a detour, not a dead-end street."
– ZIG ZIGLAR

A few important (and revealing) questions for you. Be honest. Play fair.

1. What's the first thing you do when you get new customers, beyond fulfilling the sale by delivering the purchased product or service?

2. Do you send a gift?

3. Do you recognize them in any way?

4. Do you introduce them to a referral-stimulation program?

5. Do you move them toward a higher-level purchase by offering them a more exclusive product or service than their original purchase?

If you answered *"no"* to most of these questions, you're leaving a ton of "relationship capital" on the table, and you're rejecting the opportunity to get more and better customers through the greatest customer or client-getting source of all: **referrals.** As a business owner, you need to have a solid, "post-sale" plan in place, a plan that extends far beyond the initial transaction and creates a <u>customer for life</u>, not just a customer for now.

The post-sale period is your biggest chance to impress the pants off of your customers. Send them an unannounced gift, bonus, or special offer. Do something to show that you're willing to go the extra mile and that you're thankful for their business. The more you impress them, the more valuable they become and the more likely you are to make <u>three big gains</u> instead of taking three big risks:

1. You're *increasing* the chance of return business

2. You're *increasing* the chance of referrals

3. You're *increasing* customer value.

Customer experience isn't just about your business being nice. It's also about offering other products and services and *multiplying* that one customer through continued purchases and referrals.

Take life insurance sales, for example. It's one of the toughest business models because it's so easy to make it a one-and-done sale of a policy. An insurance advisor's business is typically, just one transaction. Customers buy a policy and, often times; they don't buy another one for years, maybe decades. How do you continue to engage people who don't need your services for another five, ten, or twenty years?

That's where the top insurance advisors who are really good at what they do stand out. They do way more with their customer than just sell them a policy. They offer other, complimentary products and financial services. They might partner with an estate planning attorney, for example, and share clients, creating new income streams for one another. They might set up a sales process that moves their clients from their life insurance policy purchase to, a) Annuity presentation to, b) Portfolio Management, etc. – All things their client would be exposed to otherwise, why not have it flow to them (you)?

They will also keep the relationship alive with their client who bought a policy through a "post sale system" that might include an e-newsletter a few times per month and a monthly print newsletter, etc. to keep themselves front of mind.

All of this ads value to the customer and increases the customer's value to you – A win-win scenario. Very few create win-win scenarios today.

No one wants to work fifteen hours a day, constantly chasing the next customer. Ultimately, we want to be able to do more with less. We want to maximize the value of the customers we have now so that we don't have to work so hard to land new ones. It's been proven time and time again that it costs far more to get a new customer than it does to make an additional sale to an existing customer...

Consider the following statistics:

- If you increase customer retention rates by just 5 percent, you increase your company's profits anywhere between 25 and 95 percent.[2]

- Twenty percent of your existing customers will provide 80 percent of your company's future revenue.[3]

The Fortune Is In The Follow-Up...

For about eight years I ran a seminar business model that consisted of a live, monthly, in-person seminar held at a nearby hotel in South Florida. After my seminars, I would offer membership to into my organization which, originally was GKIC Insider's Circle (Miami Chapter) founded by Dan Kennedy and Bill Glazer. It then became my own entity, Renegade South Florida Entrepreneurs.

My team and I did two things right away for our new members: 1) we sent them a welcome gift, a box of cookies and, 2) we would invite them into my office for a new member breakfast, an orientation.

Everyone enjoys a good, old-fashioned box of cookies. It's simple, but we got more comments about those cookies than just about anything else we did because very few do it. The cookies were a blue-ribbon winner every time!

---

[2] Frederick F. Reichheld and Phil Schefter, "The Economics of E-Loyalty," *Harvard Business Review,* July 10, 2000, **http://hbswk.hbs.edu/archive/1590.html**.

[3] Lawrence, Alex, *Forbes,* "Five Customer Retention Tips for Entrepreneurs," *Forbes,* Noember 1, 2012, **http://www.forbes.com/sites/alexlawrence/2012/11/01/five -customer-retention-tips-for-entrepreneurs/#17a58c8a17b0**.

Around that time, we also sent them a copy of the book I authored with Dan Kennedy, titled *"The Ultimate Success Secret."* Basically, we showered our new members with lots of thank-you's, recognition and validation of their decision, which not only made them feel even better about their decision to join us, but also showed them that we're thorough and on top of things, that we've dotted our *I*'s and crossed our *T*'s, so to speak, and we're excited about the long-term potential of this initial transaction.

This is called, "customer involvement." The very best business models in the world get their customers involved after the initial transaction is made. The worst business models in the world fall off the face of the earth after the initial transaction is made.

Getting customers involved doesn't necessarily mean getting them involved in the business, of course. It's more about getting them involved in the *experience* of being a customer. How can you get them to really look at this new relationship as a partnership instead of a business-client transaction? How can you get them to see that a continued relationship with you can be beneficial to them in the long run?

These are key questions you want to ask yourself as your structuring your customer experience process.

Chapter 13
Creating Your
"Wow" Factor...

"Don't let the mistakes and disappointments
of the past control and direct your future."
– ZIG ZIGLAR

Think about a business that you patronized recently. Whether it was a restaurant, something you purchased from a store, or a class you took. Do you remember what you thought about after the sale was made? In just about every situation, it was probably nothing.

The company never offered you anything else, never gave you a discount to come back in, never asked for a referral, or asked you to buy something to enhance your existing product. Nothing happened to increase your value to that company or its value to you. There was no service, no experience, so it became, essentially, a "non-event" for you.

This is your opportunity to shine because so few businesses do here. Anyone can copy your products and service, but no one can be you and no one can really create the experience you create.

Zappos, for instance, does a great job of this. The online shoe (and apparel) company is famous for its customer experience and even its motto reflects that: "Powered by Service." Zappos's customer-service people aren't even called customer-service reps; they're called the Customer Loyalty Team, which reflects the overall company mission statement: to provide the best customer service possible.

Much has been written on Zappos and its company culture and how it woos and courts its customers. In fact, one of the activities the company requires of its Customer Loyalty Team members is that they send a handwritten note to an existing customer. It could be a thank-you note, a note of recognition or appreciation of the customer's value, or a note just asking how the customer is doing. It's impressive follow-up and follow-through, and it's an excellent *"wow"* factor.

Disney comes to mind too... Known as "The Happiest Place On Earth," Disney creates a "wow" experience at just about every moment it can. They are all about the experience. And, if you hadn't noticed, they are phenomenal at following up and offering you more, better, experiences, memberships and time-shares. They want to keep you in their world, make you *happy,* and of course, increase your customer value to them.

Today, more so than ever, people experience "buyer's remorse" after an initial purchase...

They buy something and then they wonder if they really need the product. Then they cancel or quit or get a refund. But if they get a small, unannounced gift with their order, or a handwritten note or something else that builds that connection, they're less likely to return the item or cancel their membership. It's about making the sale *stick* where it otherwise might not have stuck.

This goes far beyond just being nice. It's a strategy for maintaining a sale. A good "stick strategy" impresses customers, encouraging them to want to stay, do more, refer more, and find out more about you and your business and *what else* you have to offer.

Simply put… A good *"wow"* factor allows you to do more with less. It allows you to increase customer value, not just bring in more new customers, but impress the ones you've already brought in to increase their value as much as possible.

At the same time, a solid customer-experience strategy should not only serve the established customer but the prospective customer as well. If prospects don't buy now, what about one week down the road, or a month or two? In a year, if you're still staying in front of them by e-mail, physical mail, phone and text (think: multimedia) then there will come a time when those prospects *will* become your customers. If you hadn't stayed in front of them, hadn't sent offers, or continued to communicate long-term, they would have forgotten you in a heartbeat.

It really comes down to this:

You have to enforce a **Direct Response Marketing** strategy (Part 1), implement a **Multimedia Selling** strategy (Part 2), and structure a **Customer Experience** process (Part 3) or you have a broken business model. Period.

It's like three legs of a stool...

If one leg of the stool is missing, the stool tips over. If two legs of the stool are missing, the stool doesn't stand a chance. If all three legs of the stool are missing, there is no stool (aka: there is no business).

The most successful businesses in the world have these parts implemented in this precise order with a solid plan in place for each one. This is exactly the process I structure and create for every single private client of mine.

I've found that businesses that fail the fastest begin and end with Part 2: Selling. They're constantly launching into a sales pitch, throwing up all over people about their products and services, with no real thought given to strategic marketing or lead generation, which must precede selling, or major *resistance* is created. And very few businesses today, sadly, give much thought to what happens after the sale is made to increase customer value and create strong, long-term client and customer relationships...

If you have very few or no leads coming in, or little traffic to your website each week, you don't have a real business. If you don't have a sales system for moving those leads to a decision, you have a broken business. And if you don't have a customer experience and customer-service process to build a relationship with your new customer and increase customer value after the sale, you're not serious.

I know this can be a tough pill to swallow, but it can *also* be (and should be) a wake up call for you if you don't have all three parts of the Sales Velocity system in place, working together simultaneously, in perfect order.

Each of these three parts are "Assets" within your business. And it's Assets that create real wealth...

Chapter 14
Uncovering The Hidden Profits In Your Business...

"Getting knocked down in life is a given,
but getting up and moving forward is a choice."
– ZIG ZIGLAR

When my daughter was born, I remember getting ready to leave the hospital when a young lady came in with a cart holding a computer and camera, and she offered to take some high-quality, high-resolution pictures of our new baby before we left the hospital. On the computer, she pulled up examples of how we could build those pictures into cards or catalogs and how the pictures could be incorporated in a short DVD with background music.

"This is amazing!" I said. *"You can do this all right now?"* (a "wow" experience!)

One week and $220 later, these beautiful portraits arrived at our house. We'd already shared with all of our friends and family the pictures that she had uploaded onto a USB drive that day, as well as the DVD. I was blown away by the fact that the hospital had created an "upsell" process as each family left the hospital.

You'd think the hospital staff would be too busy to even think about something like this, but the numbers are probably huge for them. It's a post-sale process that creates a memorable experience for the customer (me) and is a great profit maximizer for them. No one really likes to be in the hospital, but now, new parents are leaving with the added excitement of having these amazing pictures, possibly some portraits on the way, and a DVD, all professionally done for them on the spot, capturing a most important moment.

There is no doubt that the photography company and the hospital have created a Joint Venture that benefits both of them and of course, provides huge value to each family as they go home with their new baby – A win-win-win scenario. Very smart. You can organize these types of strategic relationships to find hidden profits in your business too.

Think past the obvious. This is exactly what I push my Sales Velocity Inner Circle members to do each and every month through my advanced sales training platform.

[Take a tour at: **www.SalesVelocityInnerCircle.com**]

Game Changers...

One of the biggest "post sale" game changers for businesses is creating a residual or continuity income stream, otherwise known as a subscription-based model. Much in the same way as your utility company or your cable company does, you bill on the first of the month and in return, you offer ongoing products and services (utilities) that all come with that subscription.

Most business owners don't really think they can do this or they don't think to do this. But I promise, there is hidden opportunity here in just about every business model.

Who doesn't like the idea of selling something once and getting paid over and over again each and every month? Think NetFlix. Think Amazon Prime. Think LifeLock. But don't think for a minute you need to be a huge multi-national company to pull this off.

I once advised a credit repair attorney to create a subscription based monitoring service for <u>after</u> his initial "one-time-fee" to fix someone's credit. Think about it, after a credit repair job is done, the last thing you want is your credit to slip or be compromised again, right? So on a monthly basis for a small monthly fee, he set up a system to monitor his client's credit each month. He was essentially creating an insurance program for his clients to keep their credit in check. And, he now has a new residual income stream in place – a real <u>asset</u>.

I heard about a very successful, gourmet pizza company who sends one new gourmet pizza per month to its members who are on their subscription program. Most nutrition companies have continuity programs since you need to take supplements every day. Wine clubs as well, with their wine of the month clubs.

Costco totally disrupted the retailer space with a membership program...

In 2015, Costco revenue was $113 Billion. Membership fees accounted for a little over $2 Billion of the $133 Billion.

That's only about 2%, but they have one of the most loyal and dependable customer bases in all of retail with a staggering 91% renewal rate. And those members spend about $2,500 per year on average. They're revenue would be nowhere near that top line number without the membership model within. Genius.

The most important factor here to understand, is that most membership fees go straight to a company's bottom line. This is why you want to strongly consider continuity and subscription income as a part of your business model. Hopefully, you get the picture now and can see opportunity for yourself.

The mark of a great entrepreneur or great business model is seeing where others cannot. Like Costco did.

Another "post sale" game-changer example is simply offering an additional product or service right away that compliments the initial purchase. This is called an "upsell." Very few businesses do this. Studies have shown that approximately 20% of your customers will act on a *next* option or a *premium* option IF it is given to them. *If,* it is given to them. That's a big *if* that I know I want to participate in! And you should too.

Most are afraid to do this. That's their problem. Don't make it yours. It'll cost you a lot of money and the chance at creating better, more valuable customers or clients for your business.

What could you offer as an upsell that would add value to your customer and increase that customer's value to you, beyond the initial purchase? Think about this.

Best Buy does this all the time. You go in, buy a TV, and the employees immediately try to upsell you with a warranty or insurance plan, which is where Best Buy makes the bulk of its money, in case you didn't know.

The final "post sale" game-changer in the Customer Experience process is following through. Follow up *and* follow through. So few do today. You'll want to if you want to become a true expert and a truly indispensable option for your customers and clients.

The photography company at the hospital for my daughter's birth that I mentioned earlier actually failed, in my book…

Yes, they made a great, well thought out "initial sale." And I give them credit for that. But they dropped the ball <u>after</u> that sale was made. They got all of my information when I paid for the pictures and became a "customer" - my name, email address, physical address, and most important – my daughter's birth date!

What happened next?

You guessed it… Nothing.

What could they have done?

So, so much…

What if they left us a voucher that offered a 20% discount the next time we needed photography services? What about regular follow offering us the chance to get more pictures and videos at each stage of her development? At the very least, Email is free!

How about a package in the mail before my daughter turned six months or one-year old offering to capture those important birthday moments? Surely, there are many more, much needed photo opportunities when a baby is born...

They could have done something as simple as check in on me to say, *"Hi Andrew, we hope you're enjoying the pictures of your beautiful daughter Alessia. If you ever need more high-quality, professional pictures taken as she grows older, give us a call and we'll give you 20% off your next purchase. We appreciate your business and look forward to capturing more photo opportunities for you!"*

They could even take it a step further and spark referral activity by communicating, *"Our business grows on referrals and to show our appreciation to you for providing us with a referral, we will send you a _____ or give you a _____ for each person you send our way."* (fill in the blanks)

This stuff *really* isn't that difficult...

Then there are the other obvious opportunities such as baptisms, christenings, parties, etc. The list goes on. This photography company had the opportunity to maximize my value to them in the first year of my daughter's birth and become our "family photography company." But they failed. Because, like so many business owners today, they could not see past the initial transaction...

Why is there no *trigger* at the thirty-day mark, or the ninety-day mark, or the six-month mark to reach out to me and provide me with more value, to offer me another service? Are they too busy, too rich?

If these *triggers* are not in place in your business, in your sales cycle, why the heck not?

They could have increased my value from a $200, one-shot customer to at least a $1,000 customer *if* they had followed up and followed through. They could have done so much more with less, maximizing that one initial transaction into two, three, or four.

But I received nothing, ever. They got me at day one. And lost me at day one. It's unbelievable. But again, this is how 95% of businesses operate today. And then they blame the economy or some other outside forces as to why things aren't going well or why they're not profitable enough.

This will <u>never</u> be the case for you with Sales Velocity as your guide.

The fact is, there are hidden opportunities everywhere in your business. And it does not matter what business you are in. They're not in plain sight. They're not always obvious. But they're waiting for you to discover them, and once you discover them, it's as if you've struck gold.

Top business owners are always looking for hidden opportunities within their business. This is why they are top business owners...

Chapter 15
Pulling It All Together...

"You cannot consistently perform in a manner
that is inconsistent with the way you see yourself."
– ZIG ZIGLAR

Ultimately, *selling more with less resistance* makes your business enjoyable. You're able to attract a more ideal kind of customer or client, your business is less stressful, and you have leverage, which hopefully gives you free time to have a life…

I've laid out a <u>proven</u> three-part strategy here for you in the book. This works. This transforms small businesses into big businesses. This transforms salesmen into sales professionals. Now the tactics, the "action" piece, comes down to you implementing all three parts of the Sales Velocity formula into your business…

Part 1: Direct Response Marketing - creates the "on ramp" for attracting better, more qualified leads to your business.

Part 2: Multimedia Selling - a system for selling, utilizing a combination of online and offline media simultaneously, touching all three human senses, for maximum response.

Part 3: Customer Experience – a post-sale follow up path to increase your value to your customers and to increase their value to your business.

When you've established a foundation and a strategy for all three parts, in this exact order, you have a <u>clear</u> formula for attracting ideal customers or clients, growing your customer base and creating relationship capital?

This is the clear path to sales success. When the path is clear, speed and momentum gets created in a set, certain direction, which gives you *Velocity*. And Velocity is far more powerful than speed...

Bonus Chapter

The 2x3 Selling Method:
How To Double Your Sales Overnight With This ONE Simple 3-Step Formula...

I will almost guarantee that if you integrate this formula into all of your sales presentations and sales scripts, you will double your sales overnight.

It's a bold statement, I know. But what if I'm right?

I did not invent this formula. It is one of the oldest, most reliable direct response copywriting and persuasion formulas ever created. Versions of it have been around for decades. I've put my own touch on it, based on my twenty-years in the sales and marketing arena, and I've coined it, Th e 2x3 Selling Method.

It truly can double (2x) your sales when all three steps (3) are firmly in place. That's how I came up with "2x3."

What follows here is a transcript from one of my live Mental Toughness Sales Training Calls that I lead each month for my Sales Velocity Inner Circle members. It can be somewhat choppy at times since my words have all been pulled from a conference call. But nonetheless, and most important to you, I break the method down in great, great detail on this private call.

It's so simple, it will shock you. It's so underused today, it shocks me.

I'm <u>certain</u> it will be very useful for you as you're designing a new sales presentation or redesigning an existing one. I know of <u>not one</u> ultra-successful sales presentation that does not integrate the bulk of these concepts. Just about all sales presentations that fail lack almost all of them, so you'll want to study this closely.

Let me take you inside…

Welcome everyone…

What I'm going to show you today is the most <u>reliable</u> sales formula you will ever implement into your sales presentations. A bold statement I know. I'm going to take you through it as best I can because just having this visually in front of you when you're crafting a sales pitch, a sales presentation, a webinar, a sales letter, it doesn't' even matter, will be gold.

This will organize you greatly and it will get a lot of attention early, from your prospects. And *getting* and *keeping* attention is the key – a battle to do today.

I've heard from a lot of you that you have a team member or two that does some selling for you within your company and they're on this call. That's phenomenal, to have your team members plugging in here twice per month to expedite their training and their development.

So here we go…

If you remember from a previous training call, we talked a lot about the critical importance of getting your prospect into _agreement_ with you early on. Meaning, when you're making a presentation or you're doing a sales call or you're doing a follow up call, you don't just dive into a presentation about what you do and how you do it, you're actually making sure that the prospect gets on the same page as you so that there is instant rapport.

What a lot of novice sales people do, or old school sales people do, is they over do it with rapport and they try too hard to connect with the prospect. This happens a lot in person. They talk a lot about personal things. They try to find commonalities with family or sports or politics or whatever the case may be. Although today with politics, I don't know that that's even an option! You get the point. They try to create rapport with outside factors. This is fine to do but many take it too far.

This formula here is a legitimate roadmap for every single one of your sales calls, webinars, or in-person presentations. Anything you're selling must follow this formula, at least to a degree, or you'll face a lot of _resistance_ when selling.

Here are the three steps…

This is **The 2x3 Selling Method.** I will then break down each one of them…

Problem

Agitate

Solution

This formula originates from the direct response copywriting world. I first learned about it from Dan Kennedy. I've since adapted it for all sales funnels and sales scripts that I create for myself or for clients.

Let's Start With *The Problem...*

Very few sales presentations today deal with the *problem* long enough to get your prospect into *agreement* with you early on in your presentation...

I hope *you* agree with *me* that your product or service solves a specific problem, yes? In fact, if you aren't in the business of solving a problem, you aren't going to be in business very long!

At the end of the day, every product or service is solving a specific problem. That's really why we've created it. Whether it's information, training, a service, an investment, you name it, it's solving a problem in most cases.

What you and I need to do as sales professionals, entrepreneurs, or business owners who are running the sales organizations within our companies, is we need to be <u>crystal clear</u> on the problem at hand. I call it the "core problem" that our prospects have.

There's a level of due diligence and intelligence that has to happen here so that you really know *who* your customer is and *what* keeps them up at night.

People are generally driven by two things: Pain and Gain.

Statistically, time and time again when studies are done, the *pain* component overshadows the *gain* component by about a 3 to 1 ratio. That means that people are more driven by avoiding pain than they are by gaining pleasure. However, more than ever, we're talking just to *gain* even though we know that *pain* is a more emotional underlying factor or driver of <u>decision</u>.

I'm not saying you need to go off and create a bunch of *pain* presentations but, ultimately, if you can show someone how to avoid pain, guess what happens? They actually *gain*. It tends to be far more efficient to identify the pain points and find the core problems early on when you are speaking to a prospect.

Ideally, what we want to help them do is visualize the issue. For example, if you are getting on the phone and speaking to a prospect at some point, this is really where this works best. It also works great on webinars or live where you are presenting one-to-many.

And of course, it works super where it originated, in direct response sales copy… ;)

If you sell on a webinar, which is extremely popular today, and you don't present a big enough problem early on in the presentation, you're probably not going to get people to stick around long enough to even see your offer. And if you don't *agitate* that problem enough (which we'll talk about next), you could lose them even quicker.

The key is bubbling up the problem and making sure that our prospects are actually nodding their heads and saying to themselves, *"Yes, yes, this is exactly my problem! I'm feeling this way now. It's as if he knows me!"*

This is <u>exactly</u> what we want to elicit early on during this *Problem* phase. Too many either don't do this at all or not nearly as much as they should. If this isn't nailed down <u>early</u>, then believe me, when it comes time to present your offer (your solution) to your prospect, they will NOT be ready to receive it.

Read that again. This is a big reason why so many sales presentations fail.

Most sales get rushed today because not enough time is spent on the *Problem,* not enough time spent educating the prospect on <u>the issue</u>, which is why most sales presentations are met with major *resistance...*

Remember, to learn more about this concept and the psychology behind, "getting your prospect into agreement with you", be sure to catch the replay of the most recent Mental Toughness Sales Training Call in the Sales Velocity Inner Circle member's area.

If your prospects don't get into agreement with you that this problem even exists, you're in big trouble, and this is a mistake I see a lot of novice sales people make today, not spending nearly enough time on the *Problem*.

I was leading one of my mastermind groups not long ago, my 7-Figure Mastermind group, real successful business owners, everyone over 7-figures in revenue. One of my members just hit the **Inc. 5000 List** of America's fastest growing companies and even he admitted to not following this formula nearly enough and agreed he could be *getting* and *keeping* attention much longer and closing more deals if he drilled this into his sales team. And *getting* and *keeping* attention is the name of the game today!

I'm going to give you a quick example of some actual sales copy I pulled to really nail this for you. This was done for a company that promotes tax strategies for small business owners. I know we have financial advisors listening and I know we have accountants as well, so this is perfect.

Here it is:

"You, the small business owner are already the government's number one tax target. Every time you look at your mail, there's another tax form demanding your attention and your money. Now, you will also pay the highest price for the new tax reform unless you discover a few secrets normally used only by the big guys to fight back."

Do you see what happened in that sales copy?

The problem was <u>crystallized</u> and made <u>clear</u> right away. No tap dancing around, no weak, wimpy, sunny-day language. Right to the point, speaking right to the obvious pain.

Most business owners who are making big money, they know that they're probably a bulls-eye for a tax reform or tax hike. But often times they don't think about it or realize the seriousness of it, <u>unless</u> its put a certain way. This is the power of the right words!

This is a one-paragraph script that could be used in print or in person or on the phone. I believe they were using it with direct mail. The more and different forms of media, the better.

Lets Move To *Agitate*...

Here's where things get a bit advanced...

We all know our products and services solve a specific problem, and it's now obvious that we need to highlight the problem early on and make it clear for our prospects. But it's one thing to just mention a problem. It's another entirely to be able to take that problem and really dig in and put some *meaning* and *emotion* behind it.

(Bu the way, *this* is the mark of superior sales and marketing campaigns)

Most get a little gun shy here because they feel that injecting emotion can be viewed as somewhat manipulative. Not true. You can *ethically* manipulate without being deceptive. As the meaning suggests, you can alter someone's perception (of your product or service) by injecting emotion <u>without</u> being deceptive. This is persuasion.

Manipulation is where you try to get people to do things that they don't want to do and that they shouldn't do. Certainly not what we are after here at all.

My belief is, if you truly believe in what it is that you do 100%, and you believe that your solution and your offer is THE game-changer, THE solution that your ideal prospect needs right now, then you will be real passionate about presenting the problem and you will have no problem injecting emotion into it.

But don't take my word for it...

Just look at every single charitable organization's heart-wrenching TV commercials or direct mail packages of the suffering, scared, dying children and pets they want you to help be sending in this "tiny donation."

Major league *agitation*, big time *emotion*.

They believe so much in what they are doing to help people, they are so passionate about what they offer, that they have no issues giving you the "emotional nudge" that you need to give them money. By the way, we all need this emotional nudge to make just about all decisions we make today. It's how we're wired as humans.

THAT is *agitate*. Reject it at your own risk...

This is more or less the kick-in-the-butt that your prospect needs to ACT now and make a decision NOW. If you don't believe in what it is that you do and you're kind of half in / half out, then it might be time to look at your business model or look at maybe even offering something totally different or a different version of it because you're not "all in."

And, if you're not *all in* on your solution, believe me when I tell you, it will come across in every form of media you use to sell. I see sales people fail over and over again because they're not *all in* on what it is that they offer, not enough <u>belief</u>, so they just can't get really juiced up about it. They're not really passionate about it. They're not enthusiastic. It's a big problem, bigger than a *lack-of-skill* problem. Believe me.

When you're *all in*, and I'm assuming you all are for the sake of this call, then agitation is simply taking the established problem to the next level, digging in a bit, injecting some emotion, and really getting people to think about what it would be like if they <u>didn't solve this problem</u>.

They need to think about, and be able to visualize the consequences of how much longer they can go <u>without</u> solving this problem…

I'm going to give you another quick example here that I pulled. You can only do this to a degree on the telephone.

The example here is more of a copywriting example but again, the same methodology applies.

There's a great sales trainer / copywriter who said this. I can't remember who, at the moment. It's funny, even though it's not a funny topic. In selling life insurance and in selling funeral home services, the way he put it was:

"You have to make the customer see the hearse backed up to the door."

I know that's not lovely copy or a lovely statement but you get the point. If they can't <u>see</u> a big problem in the future, not solved, it will be difficult for your prospect to <u>agree</u>, and buy in to the problem.

Here are some *agitation* examples. This is some scripting and copy I found for a shoe company. This was written for a baby boomer audience. It's phenomenal…

"If you insist on just wearing any old pair of ordinary shoes, here's what you have to look forward to in your so-called golden years: fallen arches, intense lower back pain, extraordinary discomfort in golf or tennis shoes, even pain from just walking around a shopping mall. You'll be asking your friends to slow down so you can keep up. You'll be futilely soaking your feet at night like some old fuddy-duddy. You may even need pain pills to go to sleep."

Can you see how it paints a <u>vivid picture</u>?

If you were selling shoes and you were using a sales person on the phone, or if this were written in print, online or offline, it doesn't matter, it would be good to agitate that foot *problem* a little bit. And they do exactly that here.

It's one thing to say you have a foot problem and it may get worse as you get older, but that's kind of like dead, boring language that dies on the one-yard line. It's a whole different ball game when you talk using <u>vivid</u> examples. Visual examples of what it *could* be like if you don't solve this problem right away — Fallen arches, intense lower back pain, discomfort playing sports, even pain just walking at the mall.

This is the kind of stuff you need in your sales scripts and in your copy. This is advanced. This is what get's people to "take action."

Think about what it is that you sell now. What is your product and service? Can you think about how you can integrate emotion that supports <u>not</u> solving the problem? In it's simplest terms, it's emotion injected into <u>not</u> solving the problem.

Is this making sense to everybody?

So, *Agitate* is simply injecting emotion, adding *feeling*. So few inject emotion today. And by the way everyone... Injecting emotion is not something that you just suddenly *do*. There's a level of training that needs to happen here.

Very few know how to just inject emotion. We weren't brought up to be great sales professionals, persuasive people, understanding the power of the written word and using emotion in our sales language. It's a learned skill. There are resources that you'll need to dig into. There's studying that will need to happen for this to work for you.

We're going to be adding even more cool, new copywriting and salesmanship resources into the Sales Velocity Inner Circle member's area, but that's what you're going to need to do. You're going to need to go down this path of studying the art of crafting persuasive, emotion-driven copy or language for your sales scripts.

I'll make a great recommendation at the end, which is a very simple, go-to guide that I think will help you a lot. Again, this doesn't just come naturally to anyone.

Don't get frustrated if you're saying to yourself right now, *"I don't know what to say, this is too advanced, my customers would never go for this."*

You're wrong. You just don't have a level of training yet that's going to allow you to understand where to integrate this. Again, this is big reason why I do these Mental Toughness calls, and some of the resources I'll give you when I do these calls will really help you elevate your game in this area. And it doesn't take a lot. Very few go anywhere near using this mush sophistication in their sales presentations…

This is why only 1% or 2% ultimately succeed in sales, because they do the homework and they research and they study. I want to make sure I take you down the path of becoming a 1%er, a 2%er in your field as a sales professional.

At the end of the day, people are people. And people are wired to buy with emotion and justify with logic. Don't fight that, or you'll hit a lot *resistance* head on.

Now, The *Solution*...

This is the easy part.

The solution is what?

The solution is your product, your service, and your *outcome.* That's what it is. People don't buy things for what they <u>are</u>, they buy things for what they <u>do</u>...

What is your *outcome*? That's a key word for you here in this *solution* piece. What is an outcome that your product provides? Not just, what does it do.

For example, my product does: A, B and C, but here is the *outcome.* Here's what will happen when it's used, when you buy it, when it's integrated into your life, etc.

Here's the problem today...

Most sales professionals — on webinars, in front of a room, on a telephone call — they're too quick to dive into their *solution*. Obviously, that's logical. It makes sense, but sometimes, no matter how people got to you, not matter how informed they are when they get to you, often times they're <u>NOT ready yet</u> for the solution because you haven't dug deep enough into the problem.

Read that again.

In other words, you haven't reiterated the *problem*, and you certainly haven't *agitated* it enough by injecting emotion into the situation, where your prospect gets frustrated with <u>not</u> solving his problem, and is ready for your *solution*.

How much longer can they go not solving this?

These are the advanced psychological *triggers*, if you will, that need to be in place <u>prior</u> to your solution being offered.

Some of you may have a great sales presentation in place already, you may doing a decent job of starting off with highlighting the problem, but I would challenge you to take a *deeper* look at it to see if you're going far enough, spending enough time here early on in your sales presentation. It's so critical.

Ideally, you want to envision seeing your prospect nodding their head, *"yes, that's me, that's what I'm experiencing!"*

That's what you want to elicit. Then, and only then, the door opens (and it opens a lot more) for your *solution* — your product and service.

Problem then **Agitate** then **Solution**. In that exact order.

A *Bonus* To Take It To The Next Level…

There's one more piece here, and it's a game-changer…

I heard this from Dan Kennedy, my sales and marketing mentor for many, many years. I was actually one of the very first Certified Dan Kennedy Business Advisors in the US when the program was launched many years ago.

You don't see this mentioned in copywriting and sales training books. I've never seen it in a copywriting book, actually.

I'm giving Dan all the credit on this one. And it's a good one. This takes *problem, agitate, solution* to a whole new level...

I guess we'll call this a bonus to **The 2x3 Selling Method.**

(Thanks Dan!)

It's called: **Invalidate.**

So, it flows like this...

We have a *problem*, we *agitate* it, we move to our *solution*, and then we *invalidate*, as best we can, any and all other options (meaning, the competition).

Why is what you have so good and why should they not be looking at any other options? Of course they can look. They can do research. But, why is it that, if they do the research, you are the number one choice in your category? In other words, what is *unique* about you or your product? Why should they select you?

It's coming back at the end and *invalidating* all other options. We have a lot of options today, don't we? We have a lot of competition today, right? Of course we do!

So, what is unique about **you** that can invalidate all other options available to **them**? You want to know this. This exudes *confidence* and *leadership*. And people are instinctively drawn to confident leaders. Be one.

One of my long-time mastermind members, Josh Nelson and Dean Iodice, who own the #1 plumbing and HVAC Internet Marketing agency in the US, got to the point where they can successfully *invalidate* any and all other agencies in their space.

They did this by hitting the **Inc. 5000 List** of America's fastest growing companies in 2016. They can now use this to *invalidate* other players in their space. I mean, who doesn't want to work with the best, the recognized leader in the space, right?

But don't worry if you're not an **Inc. 5000** company. There is something about you (or your products and services) that makes you *unique*? There is most likely something proprietary, different or unusual that would help you *invalidate* all other options. You need to dig down and find it, even if it may not be that obvious. It's there.

For those of you that are more advanced and take your presentations a little bit deeper, you'll find that it <u>must</u> have these three elements in place to be effective…

Starting off with a *problem*, emotionalizing the problem (*agitate*) and then, and only then, moving to a *solution* — laying out the benefits, features, the <u>outcome</u> and the <u>transformation</u> that will take place when, not if, they move forward with the decision to use your product and service. And if need be, a little more advanced — *invalidating* all other options.

Again, why is it that you are superior? This is leadership, by the way. This isn't being cocky or arrogant. This is being really confident, "all in" on what it is that you offer so that your prospect actually *sees* that and *feels* that.

There is nothing more attractive today than somebody who is so confident about what it is that they offer, that they take a strong stance at *invalidating* all other options. They are perfectly fine in saying: *"We're definitely the best, and here's why... If you go with me (us), we're going to prove it to you."*

That's confidence. That's attractive. Even if subconsciously, that's what your prospect wants to see and hear. They want to see and hear that leadership and that confidence.

If you keep true to this **2x3 Selling Method**, it actually raises confidence. It brings you to a level of being so *organized*, that it ultimately leads to confidence, which ultimately leads to you being more enthusiastic, energetic and being way more persuasive.

At the end of the day, this Mental Toughness sales training call is about making you more persuasive. Not by making you a tough closer, but by making you a smarter than everybody else who's not getting training like this, not doing the research, so that in the end, you really don't have to sell or close. You're just taking people down a smart communication path that works, that the mind is wired to receive. Make sense?

Every human being, by the way, is wired to receive information this way. Don't think for a minute anyone isn't. Everybody is wired to avoid pain. Everybody is wired to respond more to *emotion* than *logic*.

Remember, we buy with *emotion* and we justify with *logic*, so if you're going to make logical arguments all day long, you're going to lose people. Logical arguments get made from textbooks. People don't buy from text books.

Ok, it doesn't get any more detailed than that. You have it. You have the formula. I will tell you this, and I was just running a test myself on an offer that I'm currently putting together, you want to be sure these three pieces are <u>front of mind</u> next time you craft a sales presentation.

Go back to any presentation that you're already using and just make sure that you can visually see all three (and maybe four) elements at work.

Ask yourself…

Is my presentation rigged and wired with a *problem* being <u>properly presented</u> early on?

Am I *agitating* that problem, stacking on enough emotion?

Am I then providing my *solution* — not <u>before</u>, but <u>after</u> those two triggers are in place — now that it is ready to be received?

Even if you answered "no", believe it or not, this is actually good news — good news that you <u>know</u>! Good information to have. It's only bad news if you don't know about it and you keep doing it wrong…

Isn't that the definition of insanity, *doing the same thing over and over and over again and expecting a different result?*

Unfortunately, that's what most business owners or sales professionals do today in their sales presentations, the wrong things over and again, expecting a different (better) result.

Not here. Not in Sales Velocity Inner Circle. I'll raise your game above that "mediocrity-mindset."

I guess you could say this was an "awareness call" today, to bring to your attention this method, which many of you have seen before or know already, but to break it down deeper and make sure you're all actually <u>using it</u>.

It should also trigger you to do an audit now on your existing sales presentations, sales funnels and sales scripts. And if you may be putting together a new sales presentation, man oh man did I just save you months of trial and error, money and frustration with this! Because this is the ultimate organizational tool to build an attention getting, effective, crisp presentation around these three components.

Ok, I'm out of breath. I hope you got some amazing value here today. Much more to come.

The 2x3 Selling Method is simple. It's only three pieces. Not seven, not twelve, not twenty-two. Just three. And when executed, it can easily double your sales <u>overnight</u>.

For more <u>advanced</u>, focused sales training just like this, be sure to investigate the **Sales Mastery Boot Camp** invitation I have for you on page 120. Part 1 is, *"The 7-Step Formula For Making Your <u>BIG</u> Selling Idea Stick."* Part 2 is, *"A Time-Tested Blueprint For Unleashing <u>YOUR</u> Winning Sales Presentation."*

Part 4:
Special Business-Building Resources

Not The End,
But The Beginning...

Hopefully by now you realize that Sales Velocity is a system for *elegantly* moving suspects to prospects and prospects to customers who <u>keep buying</u>.

This is (should be) the ultimate goal of every successful business. Because at the end of the day, nothing happens in business until something is sold. Plain and simple.

Sales Velocity was designed to simply serve as a "foundation" to show you how the <u>very best</u>, top-performing and top-earning sales processes are designed and built from front to back. As you read, they all lead with a compelling *Direct Response Marketing* strategy that leads into a professional *Multimedia Selling* system, in which a superior *Customer Experience* is then delivered.

I don't know that I've ever seen a highly profitable business model not operate in this fashion. That should tell you something. Again, this was the framework here, the overall strategy. Now, I want to share some advanced tools and resources with you to take this to another level so that you can implement the Sales Velocity system in your business.

Today, as Entrepreneurs, Business Owners and Sales Professionals we have to stay on the cutting-edge of what's working in the sales and marketing arena. Commitment to and investment *in* skill-development has <u>never</u> been more important than it is <u>now</u>.

Why?

Because your competition is only growing bigger, and your customer's options are only becoming more. In other words, we need to stay sharp and become sharper.

If you have the courage and the drive to step up, play a bigger game, and be different... If you dare to be great (or greater) and unlock your full potential as an Entrepreneur, then let's continue our relationship well past the pages of this book...

The ideas, people, and resources I can point you to are the very best in the world and will give you an *unfair advantage* in the marketplace.

I can only assume if you've gotten this far, this is of great interest to you...

On the following pages, I've put together a collection of hand-selected business-building resources and tools that will, literally, transform your business and accelerate your profits. Guaranteed. The first few, naturally, are from me. The rest, are from true experts and world-class organizations that I personally use and do business with. Be sure to investigate.

I look forward to meeting you one day. Hopefully, in person. Perhaps, at an upcoming *Sales Velocity Summit.*

To your success in *selling...*

Andrew J. Cass

Business-Building Resources...

Step 1: Sign up for Andrew Cass' free weekly eNewsleter, *Sales Velocity Insider*, where each week you'll get <u>ONE</u> insider secret for "Selling More With Less Resistance" delivered directly to your Email inbox.

Sign up at: **www.AndrewJCass.com**

Step 2: Sign up for Andrew Cass' *Sales Velocity Podcast* on iTunes to listen to the latest, cutting-edge sales and marketing strategies as well as hear amazing interviews with expert guests.

Sign up at: **www.SalesVelocityPodcast.info**

Step 3: Register for *Sales Mastery Boot Camp* – An exclusive 2-part training led by Andrew Cass on how to formulate your big selling idea (Part 1) and then transfer it into a <u>winning</u>, profit-producing sales presentation (Part 2). This is, quite possibly, the <u>very best</u> sales training in existence today. Invitation and full details on page 120.

Step 4: Take a tour of *Sales Velocity Inner Circle*, one of the most advanced sales training platforms in the world for professional Entrepreneurs & Business Owners.

For more information, visit: **www.SalesVelocityInnerCircle.com**

Step 5: Take a tour of *Renegade Entrepreneur University.*

Over the past eight years, Andrew Cass led a live, in-person business growth seminar in South Florida every month. Over 100 seminars in total. The very best of these training events were captured on video, professionally produced in HD quality and placed into a private online training platform, now known as Renegade Entrepreneur University, *where ordinary Business Owners become top earning Entrepreneurs.*

For more information, visit: **www.MyRenegadeU.com**

ClickFunnels: The #1 <u>undisputed</u> sales funnel software system, now with over 20,000 users worldwide. This is the one-and-only platform Andrew Cass uses to build winning sales funnels for himself and for his private clients.

Free trial at: **www.BuildMyOwnFunnel.com**

ClickMagick: A full service platform designed to track and optimize your marketing and sales funnels from front to back all in <u>one place</u>.

Free trial at: **www.TrackMySales.info**

OntraPort: Business and marketing automation software targeted to the specific sales and marketing needs of entrepreneurs and small businesses. Full service Customer

Relationship Management (CRM) platform. This is the system Andrew Cass runs his entire business from.

Take a tour at: **www.MyOntraPort.info**

The Perfect Webinar Script: A blueprint on crafting a winning webinar presentation or in-person sales pitch that has, to date, generated *multiple millions* of dollars in revenue to those who have used it.

For more information, visit: **www.UltimateSellingFormula.com**

DotComSecrets: A USA Today and Amazon best selling book with 30,000 copies sold, this is THE underground playbook for growing your company online, written by Russell Brunson with foreword from Tony Robbins. Now available for free.

Get a free copy at: **www.DotCom-Secrets.com**

The Most Incredible FREE Gift Ever: Get $633.91 in free marketing resources from the leading direct response marketing group in the world, GKIC, founded by Dan Kennedy. Includes dozens of can't-miss money-making and marketing tools to attract your ideal customers, clients, and patients.

For more information, visit: **www.GKICFreeGift.com**

A Special Invitation From The Author...

About The Author:

Andrew J. Cass was born and raised just outside of Boston, MA and currently resides in Miami, FL with his wife and two children. He attended Hofstra University in New York where he graduated in 1995 with a degree in Business Administration (BBA). He was also a member of the NCAA Division 1 Hofstra football team.

Andrew is a 20-year sales and marketing veteran, former 'Dan Kennedy Certified' Business Advisor (eight years), and co-author with Dan Kennedy in, *"The Ultimate Success Secret."* As an International best selling author, speaker, sought after sales strategist and business coach, his work has been seen on ABC, NBC, CBS and FOX.

He oversees and mentors thousands each year through his *Sales Velocity Inner Circle*, which provides advanced sales training for professional Entrepreneurs & Business Owners. Andrew also leads regular, high-level, one-on-one and mastermind group coaching specializing in lead generation and sales funnel development. Very few sales trainers and consultants today can match Andrew's long-term, experience-based track record.

He spends most of his free time with his five-year old son, Nicolas, and a two-year old daughter, Alessia. He also enjoys reading, playing golf, CrossFit training and an occasional cigar along with a Macallans Scotch.

Today, Andrew J. Cass is *still* an accomplished sales professional and serial entrepreneur. He is also a well-respected, trusted advisor to many…

For more information or to learn about speaking and consulting opportunities with Andrew, visit: **www.AndrewJCass.com**

Made in the USA
Columbia, SC
01 November 2018